TEILHARD AND PERSONALISM

TEILHARD
AND
PERSONALISM

by

ANDRÉ LIGNEUL

Translated by

Paul Joseph Oligny, O.F.M.
and
Michael D. Meilach, O.F.M.

PAULIST PRESS DEUS BOOKS

GLEN ROCK, N. J.   NEW YORK, N. Y.

TORONTO   AMSTERDAM   LONDON

A Deus Books Edition of Paulist Press, originally published under the title *Teilhard et le personnalisme* by Editions Universitaires, Paris, France.

NIHIL OBSTAT:
Rev. James J. O'Connor
Censor Librorum

IMPRIMATUR:
✝ Leo A. Pursley, D.D.
Bishop of Fort Wayne-South Bend

March 27, 1968

Library of Congress
Catalog Card Number: 68-31258

Published by Paulist Press
Editorial Office: 304 W. 58th St., N.Y., N.Y. 10019
Business Office: Glen Rock, New Jersey 07452

Printed and bound in the
United States of America
by Our Sunday Visitor Press

Contents

I
The Personalist Outlook

The human person is the focal point of contemporary concern. The threats that press heavily on him, the violations of which he is a daily victim, the alienations that disfigure him, have led to a greater understanding of his nature through the exigencies that it implies. It is not that the notion of the human person was never thought of before the so-called personalist philosophers appeared on the scene. Already Socrates, in affirming the primacy of interiority, rose up as a defender of the rights of the spiritual person.

But philosophy has a history. It even *is* history, like all human reality. Never concluded, it is openness, a perpetual questioning by man of his condition. Philosophy is inserted in the network of culture, itself swept along in the vicissitudes of history. Each era is new, unique, with its quota of particular problems. And it is through these concrete contents, this living totality that thought must turn to, that man must understand and fulfill himself.

Questions are always being raised and can never be satisfied with the answers given. There is no question whatsoever of falling into some relativism where the directing values of thought or conduct would founder, fleeting and disintegrated, in the contingencies of a moving history.

All spiritualist thought, and it is in this perspective that we place ourselves, recognizes the eternity of fundamental values. But the ideal values are the leaven which, by our action, transform reality and make it constantly transcend itself toward the realization of fuller being. Their eternity is that of a permanent call requiring an ever new response from us. And our response is situated in a precise point of space and in a unique moment of history in which it is incarnated.

Human reality, whose deficiencies are a hollow offered to plentitude, is itself in the process of becoming. It is for this reason that the recipes and procedures that a statically traditional mind would like to propose are the worst enemies of the value which is essentially a self-surpassing. "An adult does not clothe himself with the clothes of his adolescence."

The notion of person does not, any less

than any other, escape this perpetual revision. The person is inserted in the history which he helps to make, from which he cannot escape without a dissipation of his being. And to discover, brutally and tragically, that certain moments of becoming reduce the person to an unacceptable condition is to be brought to ask oneself what this person is who can mature only indirectly, by a transformation of his milieu; it is to demand an analysis of the concrete milieu in order to grasp the points of impact of a personalist action. Furthermore, it is to question oneself on the values and outstanding characteristics of the action to be undertaken. It is impossible to enclose personalist reflection in a closed system that would escape the human, temporal condition. The maturing of the person cannot be understood solely on the plane of ideas.

It is therefore urgent that we recollect ourselves in order to hear in depth those who are able to make our gaze lucid and our action fertile. The pages which follow have no other ambition than to give the reader who is not indifferent to the lot of man a zest to enrich himself by contact with two extremely prominent witnesses: Pierre Teilhard de Chardin and Emmanuel Mounier.

Personalism, of which Mounier was one

of the most outstanding representatives, is not a philosophical system. There is not "one" but "several" personalisms. It is more an attitude that branches out into nuanced perspectives, bound together by one central idea. For Mounier "every doctrine, every civilization affirming the primacy of the human person over material necessities and collective mechanisms that sustain his development is personalist." His point of departure is the existence of free and creative persons, unique subjects who are in no way interchangeable. A person is not an object, nor can he be reduced to the poverty of a concept. The real is always richer than the idea we have of it.

Hence, in some way personalism is related to existentialism; both are a vehement protest against the rationalist philosophers of the 19th century who claimed to grasp the ultimate secret of being by way of a scholarly series of impeccable reasonings. In this rarefied atmosphere, the uniqueness and mystery of persons could only be deficiencies incompatible with the clarity of the idea. Teilhard de Chardin mistrusted an intellectualism whose excess could only end in a "failure to do justice to man" (Gusdorf). "I distrust metaphysics (in the usual sense of the word)," he wrote, "because I scent geometry in it . . . Despite certain appearances, the *Weltanschauung* which I propose in no way represents a fixed and closed system. There is no question here (it would be ridiculous) of a solution deduced from the world after the fashion of Hegel, of a definitive framework of truth."

The personalist outlook is set forth, then, as a defensive reaction against every negative attitude of the human person, whether it be the misunderstanding of the real man by thought or his collapse by political, social or economic structures. This is the meaning of the courageous campaign waged by Mounier and his magazine *Esprit* since 1932.

Teilhard de Chardin can be linked with personalism. All his writings are but a sketch of a "Personal Universe." Mounier explicity referred several times to the Teilhardian vision. Teilhard brought his incomparable contribution to researches with which he very likely was not too familiar when the broad outlines of his synthesis were taking shape. He perhaps did not meet Mounier before 1946. In 1955, he spoke favorably of the magazine *Esprit*. We may then consider the development of his thought to have been independent. But does not everything that ascends converge? We have here more than a fortuitous meeting. Both explicitly appeal to Christian sources. It was their self-appointed task to make these sources come alive again and to rethink them in a language that would be effective because audible to their contemporaries. And Teilhard on several occasions characterized the direction needed to save humanity as "personalism." He was tired of seeing so many men fall back "into a traditional conservatism," and this places him in perfect accord with Mounier.

We shall find in Teilhard a concept of human personality, a line of conduct for personalist action, a vision of the future of the person. There is no need to delve deeply into the texts of this original thinker for explicit proof of our conclusions; to do so, in fact, would render this essay sterile and unacceptable. In the following pages we would like only to set forth the *main idea* of the personalism of Teilhard by showing his constant and remarkable convergence with that of Mounier, beyond their own geniuses and their individual perspectives.

The thought of Teilhard is and must remain open. He himself clearly expressed his intention: "I have no other ambition but to be thrown into the foundations of what can grow." To understand a teacher is not to repeat him, it is to prolong him. It is not to make a museum piece of him, but a leaven.

II
The Cosmic Roots
of the Person

Idealist thought had so separated spirit from matter that in the end it failed to recognize the cosmic roots of the person. Man had been defined as a "rational animal." But attention was focused exclusively on "rational." The animal was forgotten . . . But the person is incarnate, "incorporated." We do not stand before the world and view it as an object in the distance. The person sinks his roots in this material world which he transcends, but he cannot cut himself off from it without destroying himself.

Paleontology reminds us of the humility of our origins. Man entered upon the scene with noiseless tread. In body he differs little from this or that animal species that flourished at the time of his origin. Science, to which Teilhard dedicated his life, reconstitutes this slow but irreversible ascent of life toward hominization, according to Teilhard, in conformity with the law of "Complexity-Consciousness." In seeking a way to establish a hierarchy between past or present living forms, he took as his reference the progressive complexification of the nervous system, whose growth is linked with a growth of consciousness. Spirit and consciousness, however much they transcend matter, can manifest themselves only if the conditions of organic complexity are fulfilled. We have here a definitely established notion.

Furthermore, for contemporary philosophy, even of the most authentically Christian sort, the body is looked upon less as "the other," the antithesis of the soul, than as an aspect of man, forming an indissoluble whole beyond all simplistic dualism. "We found ourselves confronted," Teilhard said, "with complex grandeurs such as soul-matter . . . Now we are led to join two layers of experience apparently opposed to each other. We no longer have around us a physical domain and a moral domain. All we have is a physico-moral one." In his remarkable "Treatise on Character" Mounier reminds us on each page that the spiritual is carnal. To want to escape from these roots would be to lose one's sense of balance. "This child is abnormally lazy or indolent? Examine his endocrines before you condemn him."

One of the essential perspectives of Teilhard was to restore to man a "sense of the earth." How necessary this sort of awareness is, if the human person is to maintain his solidly incarnate existence! This preoccupation is basic in the personalist outlook, which consists essentially in a reaction to idealism's glaring inability to deal with the human person. "The cathedrals and the image-makers . . . affirm a cosmic perspective . . . which our theological literature has not always encouraged, and which has practically become lost to our sensibilities." And Mounier continued, in a note written in 1939: "Teilhard offers us an all-important suggestion . . . Let us think of that vast body which is the universe to which we are open and with which we are so closely commingled." "More and more, science and reflection present us a world that cannot do without man, and a man who cannot do without the world." When he writes: "Let us relearn the carnal meaning of the world, comradeship with things," he is saying the same thing as Teilhard, Péguy, and Claudel. The human person cannot lift himself up except by clinging to matter. It is not a question of running away from it, but of transfiguring it. For there is no complete break between the biological and the historical.

Biological evolution and the movement of history converge. History is but the prolongation of this vital élan which has prepared the way for the emergence of consciousness during the entire two to three hundreds of millions of years of the history of life. "The spiritual person is the transcendent crowning of vital evolution." He appears as "a progressive thrust toward the fulfillment of spiritual liberty." And Mounier adds: "Human progress and the movement of life are, for Teilhard, in continuity." History begins where living beings, having become autonomous persons at the time of the "threshold of reflection," take their destiny in their own hands. With man, evolution has become conscious and pursues its way under the responsibility of freedom which in this way introduces risks of failure. Agreeing with Teilhard, Mounier concludes: "With human history and behind it, there is another and more vast history—that of the universe. The world and man stand before us and both are participating in one and the same adventurous ascent."

In this way we discover that personalism is diametrically opposed to all Manicheism, to every attempt to minimize matter of the corporal. "The main contribution of Father Teilhard," Mounier wrote, "is to have restored a cosmic perspective to the Christian message." On this Teilhard commented: "The originality of my belief is that it has its roots in two domains of life usually considered mutually opposed." He intended to remain both "a child of the earth and a child of heaven." The violent attacks of Nietzsche, accusing Christians of scorning human values, or of Marx, reprimanding them for solving human problems on the plane of a mystifying beyond—these attacks lose their meaning. Man is not a being who has "fallen into the world," who has been thrown into an evil, absurd cosmos. In that case the person could fulfill himself and mature only by running away from this material world. This would be a return to the Catharist heresy which has continued down to our day in most subtle forms, particularly a strange reticence regarding carnal values. But there is beyond that the whole of the Greek tradition. For Plato, the body was only a temporary prison for the soul which is called to a higher destiny. Salvation lies in flight outside this world from which there is nothing good to be derived.

No, man is not in exile in the cosmos. Insertion in the universe is not a violence done to the normal condition of the soul, which is in no way pure spirit. We understand the vivacity of Mounier's attacks against "all the enthusiasts of the faith, with their endless, subtle evasions . . . matter for them becomes the symbol of all that is to be detested; and "materialism" is their ready epithet with which to meet anything that forces them to face the indissoluble marriage between the body and the soul, which is the heart of Christian anthropology. A negative attitude toward matter is the primary manifestation of the more specific failure to take man seriously.

We are nevertheless not advocating any sort of naturalism in which spirit is nothing more than a word. A personalism that wants to do justice to save the person must avoid this just as carefully as it must avoid a disembodied spiritualism. Teilhard does not materialize the person. He spiritualizes matter. And when he speaks of "holy matter," he does so simply to show the exalted destiny to which it is called by reason of its bond with the soul and especially, for a Christian, by reason of its divinization in the God-Man.

There is no hope of proposing a personalizing universe to man if we shatter the person in his unity. By reintroducing spirit into the cosmos, Teilhard de Chardin is doing the work of a humanist. For the hope of man "rests on a more profound conviction of the close union between openness to the eternal and a proper respect for matter . . ." Ricoeur, a personalist philosopher, clearly states that "this eulogy of matter in the dress of the spiritual, this intuition of what it means to be embodied spirit, is intimately linked with man's creative advance toward freedom. He is of one mind, here, with Teilhard, who says: "Purity does not lie in separation from, but in more profound penetration of the Universe."

In this way the meaning of Person, the meaning of History, the meaning of the Cosmos are closely connected. To grasp them is to regain the firm ground where the person feels at home without allowing himself to be imprisoned there.

Allusion was made above to the idealist philosophies in which concrete man was done away with, replaced by a game of abstractions. We now understand the traditional disdain of the metaphysician for a true anthropology. "Impatient to fasten the buckle of his system, the philosopher finding too many sciences of man and human experience too complex and difficult to follow in its real details, proclaimed that it holds no true interest." In proposing that a science of the integral man be constructed, Teilhard gives to the philosophy of the person its essential condition for existence and its best chance of success.

If man is a mystery who will always elude complete elucidation by abstract thought, this is not only because of the uniqueness of each individual wherein lies the secret of a freedom which can only affirm itself without ever possessing itself, but also because of his roots in the cosmic where matter, as such, remains impenetrable to thought, remains a sort of *limit* (which does not mean that it is not penetrated by the spirit from its very beginning, as Teilhard shows in one of his basic theses).

The need for personalist philosophy is obvious in an era in which an impressive mass of knowledge concerning man is being accumulated and yet in which, as Heidegger remarked, we know less than ever what man is. When Teilhard insistently asks that a science of man be drawn up which will succeed in synthesizing all that the individual, dispersed, specialized sciences have discovered, in order to grasp the "phenomenon of man" in his totality, that is to say, in his specificity, he lays down a preliminary condition for the construction of a philosophy of man which is also a philosophy of all of man.

III
The Eminent Dignity
of the Person

Teilhard's rich contribution to personalist research comes from his unique position in the scientific world. Personalism is turned toward the future more than toward the past. Teilhard de Chardin said many times that the past interested him only to the extent that it helped him prepare for the future. But if Mounier saw the human person as the center of reference in political or economic action, Teilhard extended the human spirit into a domain from which it had been until then excluded. With him the person became a center of reference for scientific thought. In the very name of science, thought appears as something entirely different from the ephemeral, protoplasmic accident it had been in the thought, for example, of Jean Rostand: "It may be, after all, that the development of the human intellect constitutes a case of harmful orthogenesis, like the development of the antlers of certain deer."

Teilhard reversed the situation. Now man is the key who explains the universe: "All we need is to understand man in order to understand the universe; we could never understand the universe if we did not succeed in integrating the entire man into it in a coherent way, yes, I mean all of man, without deformation, not only his bodily aspect but his mind as well." The evolution of matter and then of life, gives rise to man as its apex.

We are not dealing here with a return to static, medieval anthropocentrism, but with a "neo-anthropocentrism of movement" —not, man the center of the universe but what is much more beautiful, man the ascending arrow of the great biological synthesis." By overcoming science's relegation of man to a secondary role, Teilhard has opened to the personalist vision an area which seemed irretrievably closed. The reason is that in every field characterized by a practical dialectic between thought and action "there is no better—nor even any other —natural center for the total coherence of things than the human person."

But man, natural being though he is, is more than just a natural being. The person transcends nature and the conditions of his bodiliness. "The universe," Pascal said, "engulfs me, but I dominate it through thought." Man has moved forward noise-lessly of the genealogical tree of life. But at his birth there was an event that made him a truly new being: the threshold of reflection. For Teilhard the essence of the thought which thus emerged consists in consciousness "centering itself enough on itself to be able to grasp itself (itself and the universe at the same time) in the explicit framework of a present, a past, and a future."

As we reflect on the revolutionary consequences which this simple transformation brings to the former world-order by introducing the forces of foresight and invention, we are convinced of how ridiculous it is to look upon intelligence as an anomaly. If evolving phenomena unfold without any pause in the cosmo-biological continuity, there are nevertheless "critical points," discontinuities in the continuity where we enter into a new order. (Teilhard refused to speak of ruptures). "With man the general movement of organized beings toward consciousness has crossed a major discontinuity." A new form of life has manifested itself in nature. Man is a singular and perfectly unique being. Within himself, he finds access to an interior world. Not only does he know, but he knows that he knows. "We shall never sufficiently comprehend how radical this difference is." The spiritual phenomenon constitutes a genuinely cosmic transformation.

Certainly the cosmic nature of man is more evident than ever in this view, since this rise of consciousness is linked to a "neuropsychic mutation." But at the same time by his power of reflection—and, as we shall soon see, by his power of co-reflection —man surpasses nature; far from being a simple cog in its wheel, he is now responsible for it.

The truth is that with the threshold of reflection and the possibility inherent in human consciousness of "bending back upon itself," freedom makes man a person. The noosphere will now weave itself together; the Earth will grow new skin—better still, it has gained, in man, its soul. The inescapable process of evolution which culminates in man is followed by the movement of personalization. Man is free and his freedom has become a factor in evolution. The future has something unforeseeable about it "because of the continually growing emergence of the psychic in him, that is to say, of individual choices."

Teilhard places great stress on the fact that the evolutionary ascent never has the character of a fatal upsurge. Among other things it involves the possibility of man's refusing to go forward: "Taken individually, each human will can reject the task of mounting higher in the universe." The person does not abandon himself to the inescapable forces of matter but assumes charge of the evolutionary forces made subject, now, to his free will.

But what is freedom? It is in no wise an absolute, arbitrary freedom. In Mounier's words, it is a "conditioned freedom." It is inadmissible, Teilhard states, "to speak and to act as if a completely indetermined future were opened up to our freedom . . . We cannot strike out, with the passage of time, in any direction at all which we might arbitrarily choose." Freedom does not fundamentally consist in choosing. It is essentially the ability of a person to be himself. It is the possibility of maturing. It is an essential dimension of the person. To be free in no way means to avoid the determinisms of nature. The human person avails himself of their support in order to spiritualize them, in order to bend matter to his own purposes. He "leans" on matter, as it were, in order to conquer it, having first conquered it by thought and taken possession of it through consciousness.

The person asserts his freedom by becoming aware of his chains. For to be, to be free, is first of all to assume the datum which is mine. I assume my biological being and in this act I grasp a twofold movement that creates a tension in me: the one of personalization, the other of depersonalization, composed of all the passivities, the encumbrances which constantly tend to make me regress.

To remain faithful to the former movement, that is to say, to remain faithful to myself, presupposes that I constantly work to root out the influences which tend to hold me back. Freedom is a constant effort to liberate itself from what can alienate it. It is not possessed in the manner of a thing. It is a rejection of all that prevents the person from maturing—from following the upsurge toward being that comes from its inner depths. This is the movement of personalization which Teilhard shows as oriented toward Omega as its goal. In no way is it an unbridled freedom: this would only lead to individualism, to the worst sort of frustration. Authentic freedom is fidelity to self, to a self purified, in a word, fidelity to love. "Love and do what you will." Freedom, for personalism, is not imposed on man like a condemnation (Sartre). It is offered to him as a possibility of maturing.

But it can chart its course only by the use of abstract reasoning. The person cannot mature without effort on his part. "External structures favor or hinder, but do not create the new man who is born through personal effort" (Mounier). If freedom is an upsurge, then the person finds himself beyond himself. Teilhard could have made his own Mounier's observation that freedom "is not a sterile freedom of abstention, but a freedom of involvement." Not negative opposition but fertile affirmation.

We shall see, later, some of the rich implications of this notion of involvement; for now, let us bear in mind that Teilhard and Mounier deplored the fact that there still were so few who refused to use their freedom for their own liberation. For precisely in this and nowhere else is the eminent dignity of man to be found.

Every blow at this dignity, every lack of respect for the person, whatever its form, is deplorable precisely because the universe is thereby deprived of a certain fullness of being that this person would have contributed to it, had he himself not been prevented from reaching the fullness of his own being.

The person always remains an assertion of his own mystery in the face of every attempt to "explain" him which would claim to be adequate, as also in the face of every other illegitimate interference in his life. There is a secret in every man: the mystery of his vocation. There is something unique in every being, which cannot be alienated. The vocation of every human being is to be himself completely, and thus to play the role which is rightly his in the common effort of mankind, a role that is absolutely irreplaceable. "The unity of a world of persons can be obtained only in the diversity of vocations."

And there is always in each person more than he has contributed up to now. For life draws continually on new reserves of energy. Mounier liked to say: "To despair of a person is to make him despondent." No being has yet attained the fullness of which he is capable. There is always a beyond which we can hope he will attain with our help. And we shall soon see that a man fulfills his own destiny only by maturing within a harmonious community. Only in such a community will the person be able to experience the deep satisfaction of peace with himself: the satisfaction of obedience to his vocation.

Existence is a struggle. The person exposes himself, expresses himself, faces hard facts. He looks forward, he faces up to life. To be oneself is certainly the primary obligation of the human person; but there is no question of seeking to be singular. True originality consists in the development of one's unrealized capabilities. One can live an authentically personal life in the most ordinary conditions. Mounier mistrusted the exaltation of the "ethics of great men." He fully agreed with Kierkegaard's statement: "The truly extraordinary man is the truly ordinary man." He is, Teilhard was to say in turn, "the one who will strive to be all that he is."

This presupposes, as we shall see, that we live in communion with all other creatures. To be ourselves we must exercise our possibilities to the utmost. The person struggling to achieve a "sense of the earth" grows in this effort. In his confrontation with the forces which constantly bring the weight of risks to bear upon him, he discovers his own dimensions. This effort is personalizing. In building the world, I build myself. For Teilhard "to be is first of all to form oneself and to find oneself." And he defined what might be called the basic law of a personalist ethics: "To mature and fulfill oneself to the utmost, such is the law immanent in being." Thus the dialectic of nature opens up on the dialectic of freedom.

Even more profoundly than St. Augustine, as the following pages will prove, Teilhard gives meaning to an ethics which can be summarized in the injunction to "love and do what you will." And this ideal is not merely a prelude to purifying asceticism, but beyond it, beyond liberating detachment. Nothing will then be able to prevent the growth of the person. "The necessity of alternative phases of conquest and of renunciation in one and the same life will well up from the interior, from the depths of freedom."

IV
The Community
of Persons

The person's fundamental experience is not separation from but community with others. Individualism, that is to say, the attitude which centers the individual on himself, is contrary to the natural tendency of the person. Personalism culminates in drawing the individual outside himself and opens him to the world of persons where alone he can find his authentic being.

As I look within myself, I discover there the active presence of others. It is by their mediation—by their cooperation or by their opposition—that I am what I am. A person's emergence is the result of a constant interaction with his milieu. By constant dependence on others, with whom I bring about a community of existence, I constitute myself as an original being. I am inserted in an immense network of relationships from which I cannot escape. All existence is coexistence.

Not only is it necessary to live with others, but there are forces in me which, were it not for this coexistence, would remain untapped, needs which would be frustrated because they would find no expression for their inherent force. And because of this, my growth would be stunted. The person can only "be" by "exposing himself." To shut oneself up within oneself is never to find the road to others, is never to discover my authentic self. A stranger to others, I become a stranger to myself as well. In a word, to be is to love. I possess only that which I give and that to which I give myself. What Teilhard admirably says of "amorization" [1] harmoniously reechoes, even though in a different key, what personalists like Mounier and Nédoncelle develop with their characteristic genius.

The fundamental act of the person will then be to build up a community of persons. "The isolated man no longer thinks, no longer makes progress." We should at this point mention Mounier's profound analysis of the activities at the root of personal existence: getting outside of oneself, understanding the other's point of view, working for a common destiny, giving, being

[1] Chauchard, *Teilhard de Chardin on Love and Suffering*, Glen Rock, N.J.: Paulist Press, 1966.

faithful. All of these are acts of a community-building life.

Indeed for many, society is characterized by incessant strife. They speak of the "immense failure of the human brotherhood." There can only be a galley-slave solidarity among men, doomed as they are to the same condemnation. Sartre wrote that "hell is other people," that love is "only a mutual infection." It is true that from the beginning of history war has occupied men more than works of peace. And in our encounters, the mere presence of others very often, too often, introduces a strange opacity at the very outset of contact, heavy with defense, mistrust, calculation, vindictiveness, or worse still, indifference.

But however true all this is, it takes away none of the clarity of a different sort of evidence. A long range view shows this march of humanity through the shadows to be progressing in a direction which, as soon as we perceive it, transfigures all the data. To suffer from these insufficiencies is to realize that the person cannot perfect himself without a genuine encounter with others.

Teilhard made an inestimable contribution to personalism with his suggestion that man's future lies in the direction of a deliberately communitarian life. He sought to prove this, moreover, no longer in the name of a philosophy or of a theology, but in the name of the most certain data of paleontology and biology. So central was this insight to his thought, that for him, as for Mounier, to speak of a "personalist and communitarian revolution" would be a pleonasm.

But this transition from biological to human, according to Mounier and Teilhard, raises an important distinction between the "individual" and the "person." Personalism and individualism are diametrically opposed to each other. Let us listen to Teilhard: "Because of intellectual bewilderment or because of the intoxication of freedom, the personal molecules cannot escape the temptation of egoism . . . Man, by the very fact that he takes on individual characteristics, seems to become incommunicable and incomprehensible to others . . . and in the end he no longer perceives any other solution to his need for universal communion, which despite everything torments him, than an unconscious falling back into the faceless crowd." Thus an excess of egoist and divisive individualism causes one to fall into the opposite danger, that is, absorption into the mass of undifferentiated anonymities.

By nature the individual is *biological*. It is my material being insofar as it differs from the others. It tends toward separation. It is also a juridical term, evoking the idea of equality, of interchangeability. Individuation implies a leveling of the members of a species and a turning inward of each isolated individual upon itself.

The *person* is the individual conscious of himself, master of his actions, capable of giving himself. Persons certainly manifest themselves first of all to our experience as restricted, the finite biological units. But individuality decreases in those "units," as personality increases. Personality is at first only a seed deep within each one of us. Whereas my individuality is given to me, in the most biological sense, my person is proposed to me and my task is to finish what is still only an outline.

Mounier well says: "The person grows only by constantly purifying himself of the individual in him." This is so because contrary to the individual the person is present to himself in self-consciousness. He must not, then, let himself be drawn into isolation by his tendency to withdraw within himself. For he will not attain his fullness "by dint of self-attention, but on the contrary, by making himself open and thereby more transparent to himself and to others." This is the law of the person and of history. Teilhard made the same point as Mounier when he wrote: "The individualist ideal of '89 is outmoded."

The reason is that the crumbling, the mutual granulation of creatures into neutralized monads, is not the final stage of evolution. The history of the past brings to light the irresistible movement of collectivization which is taking shape under our eyes. The noosphere pursues its formation in an ever tighter network. Civilization, which is not a state but a process, is by nature biological; that is to say, beneath its spiritual components the influence of the vital impulse (begun some one thousand million years ago and which has suddenly entered into a new phase—civilization—with the threshold of reflection) remains permanent. Human history "only prolongs the mechanism which the animal species issues from."

There was, to begin with, a march toward individuation, through the endless game of the ramification of living forms "which, continuing in a civlized milieu," ends in persons, separate ethnic groups. A short time ago "civilization, having reached a sort of paroxysm in the West, seemed to culminate decisively in separate persons. "It was the era of liberalism, of the primacy of the individual, of the "bourgeoisie, the egoist spirit, the major obstacle of a fraternal universe."

But lo and behold! the incoercible human totalization, mounting on the horizon, comes and sweeps away the pluralistic perspective. The dream of a social milieu which would be but a springboard from which to escape in an "individualistic" solution of the problem, is over. The person finds himself confronted with another eventuality whose signs are multiplying. The wheels of unification are turning under our eyes. Two notions summarize this phenomenon: Planetization and Socialization.

Planetization

The person now lives according to the rhythm of the world, not of the village. The compression of peoples who are being brought more and more closely together produces an economic and technical organization where energy is unified. Intellectual organization, which is being increasingly encouraged, issues in more extensive knowledge of the world. The human race is thus deploying itself at an increasing rate into a structured, thinking whole.

The person is inserted in a planetary network which makes him both a part of and responsible for the totality. "Reflection planetizes" by integrating us physically and mentally into the universe of mankind. There is no longer question of considering oneself French or Chinese but as "terrestrial." "The true man is he who gathers together in himself the consciousness of the entire human stratum." The organization of the planetary community prolongs evolution, and the latter then overflows into the psychic organization of the planet.

Socialization

The graph of the development of humanity shows that it is approaching its critical point of socialization. The reason for this is the spatial limit which turns mankind back on itself. To be sure, terms such as "socialization," "collectivization," "compression," awaken unfavorable resonances in us. They immediately call to mind a sort of repression of free persons. It is easy to stress "many disquieting symptoms" in this progressive vice-hold. "Fear of levelling, under a layer of neutral culture, differences which have brought about the rich variety of human productions; fear of losing our ego in the anonymous mass; fear of the person in face of a blind machine, the subjection implied in mechanized work; fear of a world of termites, of collective monsters, "heartless and shapeless Molochs."

The personalist movement was born precisley to resist the threat to the person and personal values raised by all these processes of collectivization, in which originality and personality, are too expensive a luxury, in which individuals abandon themselves to anonymity and irresponsibility. But how can one react when faced with this irresistible pressure? Man is not an insect, as Teilhard put it. Nothing is more pathetic than the blind devotion of an ant to his ant-hill. That would end for man in "the annihilation of our personality." But in any case "the elements of the noosphere, in virtue of their spiritual nature, are not exactly comparable to anonymous and interchangeable corpuscles."

Man is free, he thinks, he is responsible. The problem, therefore, is to hominize this transformation. For it is impossible—it would be deadly—to close our eyes to this irresistible determinism which makes humanity contract on itself. It is a question of controlling it and making it issue, not in the suffocation, but in the maturation of persons. "The union will be effected in any case. It depends on us whether it be for the dissolution of the ego or for its completion."

We have reached the limit of progress which can be achieved by individual effort. And the moment when "for the first time men are becoming conscious not only of their growing interdependence but still more of their marvelous unity (Pius XII), it is easy to see how the progress of the human person is linked to those of "the psychic organization of the noosphere."

If there is a danger, personalism chooses the danger. First of all because this movement, we said, is unavoidable: we cannot escape socialization. Secondly, because on the contrary, it is not at all inevitable that it militate against man. Thinkers that we could not suspect of denying spiritual values, such as John XXIII, recognized this. It is up to us to see to it that the "collectivization of the Earth is carried out and that it unite us in a common soul." "We cannot climb a mountain without skirting an abyss." It will succeed if it takes place under the sign of love. And if we know how to look beyond appearances and discover the current of life which is constantly triumphing, we perceive a convergence which structures it in depth.

Since, on one hand, humanity is converging and, on the other, man possesses an essential communitarian dimension, we may be thoroughly optimistic regarding the outcome for the person in this contraction of humanity. "Whether we want it or not, the age of lukewarm pluralism is definitely over. Either one people will destroy and absorb all the others or all peoples will group together in one common soul in order to be more human."

Violent conflicts will still accompany this planetary unification. Every new stage is marked by a crisis of growth. We go in fact from divergence to convergence, and the world that is born must shake off the weights of the one which is disappearing. But this compression on self, by enhancing consciousness, will be ultra-personalizing. "The most humanizing of moral dispositions we know of is team-spirit." More and more men are discovering that they are made to collaborate in a common work. History shows a joint ascent without which the summits would not be what they are, were they completely isolated from the community.

We can avoid the baneful effects of socialization, if we know how to make use of reflection—better co-reflection. By developing his communitarian dimension, the person deepens his own existence. Just where the individual thought he had disintegrated, the person will find himself enhanced beyond all his hopes. For "union differentiates."

Union personalizes through the gentle influence of internal forces of attraction, not under the pressure of external forces of coercion. This totalization differentiates what it unites, that is to say, procures for each one his optimum fulfillment and uniqueness. But only the unanimization resulting from the participation of each freedom will lead to a personal universe. The more persons are deliberately communitarian, the more the collective forces will function conformably to the structure of free elements. Whereas the resignation of men, their fight from common tasks, would only leave forces of gravity free to work for the annihilation of the spiritual. There is on all these points the most complete agreement between Mounier and Teilhard.

To withdraw before this ascent of socialization would be a biological regression, whereas the person, by participating fully in the ascent of humanity, would carry his unrealized capabilities to the maximum of development. In this way he would reach full maturity, whereas in isolation he could look forward only to sterility. Each one's fulfillment depends on the fulfillment of all. Humanity enriches itself by the union of differences (of persons or groups). Just as in a more complex organism the organs and functions are better differentiated, so also in a more centered and more organized humanity, every conscious center will enjoy a more intense personality, far from having to fear a stultifying uniformity. Indeed, union differentiates.

Teilhard benefited from the experience of a scientific team where the cooperation of minds united in a common venture showed them to be capable of obtaining results impossible of attainment of isolated researchers. And nevertheless each one only became more himself. Union procures more awareness, more knowledge, a greater radius of action, more freedom.

For personalist thought, the most precious values of interiority are not necessarily endangered by exposure to the fresh air of communal living. Mounier saw in the authentic encounter of others the condition of one's own authentic affirmation. To encounter another is to see in him something else than an instrument at my service, a "wholly other." It is to open myself to him, to meet him in myself, in a word to love him. This openness whereby the other enriches me with his own values presupposes that I have recognized those values.

Love, the highest form of union, is the

creator of distinction and of harmony. To
love is to summon the other out of his soli-
tude. And if this gesture frees the one sum-
moned, it likewise liberates and enhances
him who summons. Love is the strongest
affirmation of the person. "The personal
man is not a desolate man. He is a man who
is surrounded, swept along, and called."
Thus, others are in no way an obstacle to
the person, but on the contrary indispensable mediators. For the community is not
born of the obliteration of persons, but of
their fulfillment.

If the person is defined by his vocation,
the community is defined by a common
end. And partial communities have to
struggle constantly against their degrada-
tion into closed societies, refusing to open
themselves to the "planetary sense." We
will thus cooperate in "the parallel restoration of the community and of the personality." This is Mounier's explanation of the
differentiation achieved through union.

At the level of consciousness, we have a
presentiment of what the nature of that
energy is which quickens this growing
ascent. If the excess of individualism entails
a catastrophic dispersion of efforts, the reason is that it forms an obstacle to this dynamism. "Since in union everything is

moved in and through the personal," Teilhard tells us, "love necessarily forms the stuff of human energy."

The latter manifests itself to consciousness at three levels of spiritualization: sexual, human, cosmic. More profoundly, it takes its roots in divine love which maintains this evolving universe in existence. "It is a love which physically constructs the universe" and to it finally are brought back all energies. Love, in Teilhard's sense—the physico-moral energy of personalization—is a general property of all life and as such it espouses in varieties and in degrees all the forms taken successively by organized matter."

Teilhard shows his sympathy with the mediations of a personalist like Nédoncelle when he writes: "Love alone is capable of uniting living beings in such a way as to complete and fulfill them, for it alone takes them and joins them by what is deepest in themselves." It suffices, to reconcile the person and the universe, to imagine "that our power to love develops itself to the point of embracing the totality of men and of the earth." And this socialization, that is to say, this union of men into an ever more universal, ever more organized, society, will be an "amorization," that is to say, an impulse quickened by love and overflowing into an absolute Love.

For men, there is only one way to love, only one way to show love for one another: it is to orient each man toward the same center, which alone can bind us together even as it gives to each of us the plenitude of his own personality. The high point of Teilhard's vision is his certitude that "each Ego is destined to attain his fulfillment in some mysterious Super-Ego." Life and the universe are converging toward a personal world. But for this convergence to be personalist, it is required that it be directed toward a supreme person.

Very early in life, Teilhard was preoccupied with what could give consistency to fugitive realities. All his life he was oriented toward the One who would assure the multiple an emergence into eternity. No personalist thinker, in fact, can avoid experiencing the incomprehensible need of assuring the person a foundation on which he can find an absolute support. Thus, it was through his personalist outlook that Teilhard found the Christian Absolute, even though he had possessed him in the faith of his childhood. There are many roads leading to God; each conscious person must achieve his own individual encounter. For Mounier, as for Teilhard, God appears as the answer to a need arising from their vision of history or of the universe, rather than as a *tour de force* added to their vision to satisfy an extrinsic need.

And the sense of the community, the capital importance of which we have seen, is itself subordinated to that of God. Humanity is converging on itself, first of all. But the common action which results from this movement needs to orient itself in turn toward a center, a real center, where its aspirations can be satisfied in order that the fullness of reality it has attained may be saved from ultimate failure and transfigured. For the progressive fusion of minds, which is to culminate in the formation of the noosphere, can come about only if they tend toward a common Center. This Omega, this Center of convergence, cannot be less real than ourselves.

We cannot picture Omega to ourselves as a potential synthesis arising simply from the fusion of the elements it gathers together . . . It can only be a distinct Center. Neither can it be a center that "would annul in itself" the person it has united, as would the Absolute of Vedantic Thought, incompatible with the existence of relative beings. The notion of person no longer makes any sense in this latter perspective, since the individual self would be only illusory and the transcendence of self of which it speaks is a total fusion in a massive Absolute lacking all distinction.

The Absolute of Christian personalism, of Teilhard in particular, is a Personal Center who will bring every individual center, constituted by concrete persons, to its highest degree of personalization. It is this ultimate pole that will bring human persons to perfect maturity precisely through its freedom (due to its transcendence) from "the fatal regression which threatens every construction of stuff of space and time."

The person can perfect himself only if he encounters at the term of his becoming a personal union, without risk of confusion between the two beings so united. This Omega, the ultimate term, God, is also, for Teilhard, the Christ, the God-Man whose return at the Parousia will complete the plenitude of the universe of persons. This Center, ever before us but already present, will gather together and consummate what is most essential, most incommunicable in each element reflected in the universe. It enables the human person to avoid every danger of disintegration by regression.

The energy that quickens the universe is Christic (and in this Teilhard has rediscovered the authentic teaching of St. Paul); that is to say, it makes the universe participate intimately in the growth of the Mystical Body, in mankind's progress through history. Cosmogenesis is also christogenesis. Pius XII wrote: "For the first time, men are becoming conscious of their marvelous unity. This means that humanity will always become more disposed to become the Mystical Body of Christ." In the domain of human progress, Christ appears as the One who makes evolution surge toward the higher destiny of divinization. "All things were created through him and for him" (Col. 1, 16). Inversely, Teilhard asked, "would the Parousia be possible without the continual work of every human cell to unite with all the others?"

Thus, man is communitarian, as much for biological reasons as because of a call from beyond himself, a call from the future, a call designed to enhance his freedom. And if the community is an essential dimension of the person, "love of neighbor essentially presupposes . . . that men can, in a real and physical way, recognize themselves in one another, as members of one and the same being for whose appearance all of them ardently yearn."

Interiority, then, characterizes the person; and it is by this conversion to interiority that the person fulfills himself. God, the source and center of all beings, is ulti-

mately in the deepest recesses of consciousness. The interiority which is the spirit
opens itself for the Personal Spirit. But it is
no longer a return to interiority which
would isolate from the community or
would cut the person off from nature. On the
contrary, it is a gathering together of self,
the ultimate term of the becoming of every
element.

If the movement toward others is the ini-
tial step, a return to self is its complement.
The person disintegrates in an external
tumult if he loses the ability to pull himself
together, to gather himself up in a center,
to unify himself. Mounier places great emphasis on this point. "He must freely recover
this movement of centration, of unification
which had prepared its coming even to
the threshold of reflection." Recollection,
which is but a temporary retreat, is justified
by the need to replenish our energy for a
more effective advance.

The fulfillment of every man's vocation
definitely presupposes this recollection or
temporary retreat. We need to discover in
ourselves the call toward this living one-
ness: unity within ourselves, union with
others. We must hear this call and allow it
to stir up in us a resolve powerful enough
to overcome both interior and exterior obstacles to our progress. The interior obsta-

cles (most formidable of all) are all those passivities which tend to induce inertia, and it is only in recollection that a liberating ascesis can take form.

Recollection means first of all the gathering together of energy which of itself would tend toward dissipation. To recollect oneself is to make this energy converge toward the realization of fuller being. For personalist thought, it is in effort and in obscurity that we experience this call, this vocation. To the extent that we participate in the common work, the true meaning of existence, of each of our own individual existences, unveils itself to our interior gaze.

V

The Involvement
of the Person

The person, having become fully present to himself through reflection, has become responsible for himself and for the task of continuing the élan which brought him into being. He is thus called to "respond," to prove himself by "becoming involved." "The real test of a man is his actions," Mounier affirmed. The term *involvement* has a twofold meaning, both that of a man who has embarked on a destiny which he has not chosen, and the incomparably superior meaning of a man who "involves himself" by a fully free initiative.

Teilhard felt keenly the urgency of presence to a world that has reached a new stage in its becoming, a stage however that bears the appearance of a crisis. He echoes Mounier when he writes: "A civilization begins to preach action when its power to act wanes." The refusal to act as well as action for action's sake is devoid of sense. On the other hand, action without an open perspective on transcendence, action in a basically absurd world, can only end in despair. Activism is only disorderly retreat from action. It is delirious to grant a charter to "any action whatsoever provided it be intense." In order to be, therefore, the person involves himself, but he knows what cause he devotes himself to, and the justification of this cause justifies him who takes it as an end. In this very way, the person fulfills himself.

There is no true involvement without reference to an Absolute. If man is man only by involvement, he is more than his involvements. And this Absolute who quickens his actions and assigns limits to him, assures him of this necessary transcendence. For Mounier, as for Teilhard, "the end of the action is to modify the external reality in order to build, to bring men closer together, to enrich our universe with values."

Teilhard has shown us how much this building of the earth, of the New Earth which personalism calls for, has taken root in the very depths of cosmic and spiritual exigencies. Evolution overflows. It takes place at the level of spirit. To be is primarily to accept being; to assume the human condition is to accept the involvement of transforming it in its painful struggles. The tragedy lies in the distance which separates us from the Absolute whose presence is not given us in its fullness. But we are "launched," that is why abstention is illusory. Humanity "si faradà se," Mounier liked to say. "Why evolution, why the hesitating march of history? ... God has willed that the liberation of man be the fruit of man's work, of his genius, and of his suffering ..." And he summed up in this way the command by which he revealed his plan to man. "Be in the world as if not being in it, but *be* in the world." This is another expression of what we have called a "sense of the earth."

Mounier speaks "of a long series of regressions," such as romantic nostalgia for the past, bourgeois conservatism, etc. ... regarding which Teilhard has written some passages in which the serenity of expression ill-conceals an indignant impatience with all those who avail themselves surreptitiously of every pretext for avoiding progress. Man can refuse to advance. The ever-present evil is the person who "ceases to go forward," remarks Mounier: the person who allows himself to be alienated by the weight of matter no longer quickened by the spirit, by the interplay of political or economic structures which have lost his soul.

Certainly, as they face a world in process,

many are seized with fear. The evolution of the sciences, of technology, of cybernetics, has put man in possession of an ever greater power, and yet "never has the feeling of fatality and of our powerlessness been stronger than in this world which offers us the means to power." So true is this that "the world appears to us, in the perspective of our age, as a history of fools . . . Man has lost his mastery of the universe he has formed, he sees himself madly drifting toward events which he no longer masters."

But there is a way out. Mechanization has been violently attacked in the name of man. Mounier, in some well-known passages, analyzes the anti-machine myth and in the end shows it as a manifestation of the fear of change. For him it is an "infantile reaction of incompetent and panic-stricken travelers . . . a reaction of a disconcerted child, a loss of composure before a suddenly enormous responsibility." And yet, as we have seen, the movement of history is irreversible. We must act. Only one way is left. Teilhard, in his turn, points it out to us. His first step is to "see." "Make the effort to see."

Let us look with completely new eyes, eyes worthy of a young earth, at this world built by man's hands. We impugn it as artificial. But is not man the artifice, Mounier asks? Teilhard likewise speaks often of "all that is natural in the heart of artificial man." The superiority of man lies precisely in the power to create his milieu. Moreover, the process of the artificial is closely joined to that of the technology. All personalism owes it to itself to take a firm stand when faced, alas, with what all too often reveals itself as a source of alienation for freedoms.

Technology is ambiguous. Technical progress is never neutral. "Does not the new world, instead of effecting the hominization of nature by man through the machine, run the risk of involving the objectification of man by the machine?" Teilhard, for his part, would envision the possibility of society "invincibly mechanizing itself." But if technical progress "can lead to disaster, it is precisely because it opens up the most lofty possibilities."

Mechanization, in itself, is ambivalent. But it is a condition of the future of man and a factor of hominization. "The machine can be a march toward the freedom announced in the Scriptures in which man will reestablish his sovereignty over nature at the same time as his inner unity." By proposing an authentically effective personalism, Teilhard echoes Mounier in offering a genuine humanism. It is in the name of spiritual values that both acclaim "the

sudden and irreversible ascent of the industrial phenomenon," for the machine leads
man toward "a maximum of consciousness
with a minimum of effort." It liberates him
"from the crushing weight of physical and
mental work." It increases "free energy . . .
The freer man's head is the more he re-
flects." Mounier shows how the person is
open to ever new cultural development by
modern communications media.

It is indispensable to recall that every
mystique demands a technology if it is to
capture the world's attention. Could it be
otherwise? It is "all the same impressive to
see the geographical extension of Christianity coincide with that of technical civilization," Mounier remarked. We perceive
how the reconciliation of man with nature
is an aspect, a condition even, of the reconciliation of man with himself and with God.
For Pius XII "it is undeniable that technical progress comes from God and therefore
can and must lead to God." For the transformation of man presupposes, among
other conditions, the transformation of the
milieu. Yet, this demands that technology
be quickened by a mystique. For it is less on
the general raising of the level of life than
on the faith of man that "the ultimate success of failure of humanity depends."

Production has value only by reason of

its higher end: the emergence of a world of persons. But to those who see in technical developments the enemy of the person, Mounier answers that this progress "develops one of the essential aspects of the Incarnation and perfects, on one level, the very Body of Christ."

Furthermore, although Teilhard's humanism is a scientific humanism, it is radically distinct from any scientism which would resolve all the problems of man with only those resources and methods valid in the domain of matter. It is scientific in the sense that science plays an essential if subordinate role in it. We have just seen, e.g., its influence implicit in the development of mechanization. But scientific research itself has a personalizing value.

Let us note first of all that it is a question of science as Teilhard conceives it: not a knowledge that remains on the level of the analysis of, say, physical particles, but a research which tries to attain a global vision of that totality that must indeed be analyzed if our knowledge of it is to bear practical fruit.

Science, for Teilhard, is "phenomenology," of which he gives us an inspired illustration in the *Phenomenon of Man,* a science that gives man his rightful, preeminent place. Science is then "a form (and one of the most perfect) of what we call being or life, or evolution. We cannot define the world in any other way than by a gradual awakening of consciousness . . . Scientific research has the very value of the universe which is developing in each one of us." That is why nothing can nor must ever "prevent man from an unceasing effort to think of everything and give expression to everything."

The mystique of science, for Teilhard, is something entirely different from materialism. Scientific research is part of man's fulfillment. Mounier shows how a rejection of science in the name of spiritual values, is an unprofitable, anachronistic attitude. "There is less difference than we think between research and adoration," Teilhard tells us in a text which at first sight surprises us, but which is only another expression of his conviction that all creation has been taken up in a movement of divinization.

Furthermore, since man personalizes himself by increasing his communitarian dimensions, science is a factor of unanimization. The scientific team or the group of researchers—there are no more independent ones—is for Teilhard the model of humanity "cohering in itself" and by that very fact augmenting its degree of consciousness.

The person is, therefore, engaged in this transformation of the world, the condition of his own transformation. He is responsible. This is one of the major themes of personalism. "Nature is not only the womb of humanity, it is ready to be recreated by man . . . Man today knows that he is called to become the demiurge of the world and of his own condition." This is what Teilhard so rightly called "the surge of evolution" on the level of the noosphere. The man who believes in evolution—Mounier would say: who believes in the meaning of history— "sees the grandeur of his responsibilities almost infinitely exalted before his very eyes."

The success of the immense travail of the universe is in the hands of the least of us. Our part in it, however small it is, is nevertheless very real. Responsible for self, responsible for humanity, responsible for the use of his power, such is man quickened with the sense of the world and of the meaning of his spiritual destiny.

We saw above that "the more we seek to promote the progress of the world, the more will we take an active part in the march of the world toward God." Work, therefore, is an undertaking of the spiritualization of matter and of the person.

The question of work is necessarily at the center of the preoccupations of the personalist thought. Perhaps it is precisely because work and its conditions are so repugnant to many men today that they constitute the point of impact of a "personalist and communitarian revolution." This epithet of Mounier is equally characteristic of Teilhard. He was keenly conscious of the need to rescue genuine human labor from its unfortunate role as a cause of dehumanization for the majority of those who give themselves to it. He has a philosophy, even a theology of work. The latter is characterized by a splendid framework of values, beginning with the relationship established between cosmogenesis, anthropogenesis, and Christogenesis. His entire essay, *The Divine Milieu,* is pertinent here, with its insistence on the matter-soul-divine triad; "whatever we do, we bring back to God a part of the being he desires." Matter is spiritualized by human effort, by work. In this perspective, the person again finds a taste for work, and at the same time new strength to transform the conditions of industrial work and make them humanizing and no longer crushing for the person.

Man is responsible for the world that is being born. Work is its condition, but not its ultimate end. It will always be laborious, but if it is accompanied by a deep, creative joy, it makes possible the fulfillment of the person, whereas a mystique of production abolishes every idea of dignity. The reader is doubtless acquainted with the numerous passages in which Mounier and Simone Weil deplore at length that mechanical, assembly-line kind of work which is done without joy, where work is reduced to merchandise, the only value capitalistic liberalism knows. The work of Mounier will remain one of the most representative of personalist reaction seeking to restore to work its true image.

Moreover, the community of work creates deep bonds between its members and prepares them for fruitful participation in larger communities. Among the essential communities, Mounier places the trade unions where the workers become more keenly aware of their human dignity and of the inroads made on that dignity, with a view to regaining it by cooperative effort. Teilhard did not actually deal with these problems. But the concern he showed, not only for those who suffer but for those who are victims of unfair trade practices—and concern is but an essential form of charity —certainly shows the implications of his personalist outlook for this important area of human affairs.

For the restoration of matter's rightful value—and matter for Mounier was "divine," "holy" for Teilhard—personalism has repudiated the idea of physical labor being linked to a corruption of human nature. For certain masters of the spiritual life, work was a means of forgetting self and found its value in the right intention which animated it. In itself it was of little value. Its consecration remained external to its content, to its results which remained secular. With the sacralization of all reality animated by divine love and oriented through transcendence toward Omega, work became intrinsically spiritual and thereby personalizing.

Personalism is an efficacious humanism. We spoke of revolution, that is to say, of a seeking for efficacy. "Let us save humanity." This is an appeal to the formation of an "advanced human front." The messages of Teilhard, of Mounier, of personalism, keep telling us that "nothing is worth the trouble it takes to find it except that which has never before existed. The only discovery worthy of our efforts is to build the future." These words are thoroughly typical of Teilhard, who had no interest in the past for its own sake but only insofar as it enables us to lay the groundwork for the future. This can only be our work, the work of all, for the Earth needs all its blood, that is to say, the blood of each individual, no matter how insignificant he may appear to be. As we set about building this new "City," moreover, we shall need a clear grasp of the obstacles in our path, for "in every field it is at the moment when the old framework is about to be shattered that it offers the greatest resistance" (Teilhard).

Flight from reality in the name of a pseudo-purity and the interior evasion of the enthusiasts "are infinitely easier than efficacious involvement." Scorn or ignorance of the temporal responsibilities of the person are the fruit of a poorly informed faith. It is against this insipidness that Teilhard and Mounier raised their voices. "God is reached through human success." We must transcend the opposition of contemplation and of action, too often stamped with the bankruptcy of an interior life that remains isolated in bitterness and narcissism. The taste for contemplation must not be used, as it often is, to cover up for a cowardly flight from human life.

Let there be no mistake. Teilhard does recommend that we throw ourselves recklessly into action: that we first attach ourselves to the world, but this first phase takes all its value from the second, with which it is intimately joined, i.e., from a genuine detachment which is the necessary condition for progress. This detachment demands a perpetual transcendence of everything that might immure a person or group of persons in out-of-date, hardened structures which would be incompatible with the greater perfection to which they are called. "This detachment makes us indefinitely free, always open to the possibility of attaining new richness of human existence. Once this conversion has been accomplished, "what freedom to work and to love!"

Action, too, can alienate us, especially when it becomes action for action's sake. To seek God in everything is, by definition, to attach ourselves to nothing definitively; and in the same act, "unbelievably rich and simple, the spirit of detachment and the spirit of conquest . . . combine to correct and exalt one another." This is not a Nietz-schian attitude which would be only a glorification of brute force; the subordination of technique to a mystique requires an arduous ascesis. The labor of the "good worker of the earth" is a factor of detachment to anyone who gives himself to it with docility. "It implies effort, the tension involved in creation, and it purifies one of the vice of egoism and of complacency."

Further explanation is needed. If lethargy is the capital sin, strength will be the essential virtue of a personalist morality. Morality, Teilhard tells us, has too often been solicitous "to maintain a static equilibrium between individuals by encouraging them to place undue restriction on their energy, i.e., on the force of evolution." But "to attempt everything and to push everything to the very end in the direction of the greatest consciousness (that is to say, of love), such is the general and supreme law of morality in a universe which we recognize as being in a state of spiritual transformation: to place limits on the force of evolution (except as a means to enhance it)— that is sin."

It would be wrong to equate this position with Nietzsche's glorification of power, and his exhortation to cultivate an unfeeling obduracy. This would be to forget all we have said about love-energy. This force of which Teilhard speaks is none other than the force of amorization because, for Teilhard, love is the highest form of human energy. He knows very well that power, in the usual sense of the word, is terribly ambivalent. But he also knows very well that love without force is nothing more than sentimental reverie. He is one with Mounier in condemning traditional morality as "a poison for young muscles."

When fully attaining human stature is involved, we must reject a code of propriety the principal concern of which would be to discourage even the proper channeling of our legitimate impulses. In a word, Teilhard urges us to avoid acquiring a taste for "virtues crowned with poppy." Morality is not a code of prohibitions, it must first of all be a source of dynamism. It is exactly the opposite of what it would be if it placed a fear of energy at the heart of its ascetical ideal. For in that case it would be but a mortal opium for the evolutionary élan.

Nietzsche's intuition was not wrong when he excoriated certain deviations of Christianity for turning away from life, for being only a spineless sentimentalism. "Because a rooster crowed too loudly, they demand that there be only capons." It is in response to Nietzsche that Mounier and Teilhard elaborate a morality of force, but in an entirely different atmosphere. The latter, for example, asked himself "how he could reconcile as effectively as possible a legitimate concern for the wounded and the more important demands of the offensive. In what does true charity consist?" The solution certainly does not lie in stiffling human energy, but in its direction toward a higher end. "An ever greater excess of free energy, available for ever vaster conquests, this is what the world expects from us and what will save us."

Love is a combat; life is a struggle against death; the spiritual life is a warring against the inertia of matter and the tendency of life to take refuge in sterile slumber. "The person becomes conscious of himself, not in an ecstasy, but in a dialectical interplay of forces. Energy is one of its principal attributes."

These descriptions of Mounier are identical with those of Teilhard. The ambiguity found by many is due to a tendency to understand force in its most barbarous form: war. But the true successes of force lie elsewhere. There is an evident analogy here with the dialectic of "involvement-non-commitment," which we have already discussed. It is a matter of possessing force without being dominated by it. Mounier admirably shows that this return to a virile vigor is totally in keeping with genuine Christianity. To be is to love. It is also to affirm oneself, in the very name of love.

VI
The Person
and Time

The transformation of our attitude toward matter is bound up with that of our understanding of time. Meditation on temporality and its implications for the destiny of the person is fundamental for personalist thought. Temporality, historicity, is essential to all that is subject to the uninterrupted movement whereby the future becomes present and the present past. It is characteristic of everything which endures yet changes. All present-day anthropology necessarily implies historical perspectives, and Teilhard therefore rightly places strong emphasis on time, which has been rediscovered, as it were, in its central importance by the modern world: by the exact sciences as well as the human and social sciences.

Every type of personalist philosophy thus tries to take into account the various philosophies of history which seek to understand the succession of events. Teilhard won-

dered, as we have seen, what mode of relationship to the earth, i.e., to temporality,
the man who wishes to be an authentic person must pursue. Now, the value and the
fulfillment of the person are linked with
those of time. In atheistic existentialism, for
example, or in Hindu thought, sheer temporality bereft of value offers no challenge
to human life. All that remains is absurdity
or illusion; there is no longer any place for
the person.

The rediscovery of the sense of duration,
of history, is characteristic of the 19th century, a period of lively reaction against a
static ideal of life and against the concept of
eternal truth frozen in a kind of atemporal
absolute. "Today, the positive knowledge
of things is identified with the study of their
development . . ." To our newly opened
eyes, each element of things is henceforth
extended backward and tends to pursue itself forward, endlessly. It is scarcely necessary to point out how the discovery of biological evolution contributed to this change
in perspective.

We have already seen how the person is
the summit, the spire of all antecedent evolution, and how progress continues in the
evolution of the noosphere. Teilhard
quotes this statement of Breuil: "We have
only just cast off the last moorings which

held us to the neolithic age." Mounier said in similar words: "Humanity is closer than we think to its uterine life." The future is opening up before us, and it is immense. We are enveloped in duration. "The universe has always moved, and at this moment, it continues to move." We are familiar with this famous passage from the *Phenomenon of Man*.

There is therefore in Teilhard a philosophy of history, that is, a reflective view of its nature and direction. He constantly fought against a static view of the world which, as we can easily see just by looking at the evidence, is catastrophic by its disregard of movement. But actually this philosophy is not peculiar to Teilhard; it is the Christian philosophy of history, which both he and Mounier have helped to elaborate. His originality, we have seen, lay in linking the historical more closely to the cosmic, and the advent of the City of God to that of the earthly city.

The notion of progress, so dear to the 18th century, was simply the biblical idea of the march toward the Messianic era, but cut off from all religious and transcendent perspective, and thus deprived of all foundation. The person can, in truth, fulfill his being only if he gives due attention to his cosmic roots, but he can attain his fulfillment only in an eschatological transcendence. Time needs eternity to escape annihilation. The Hebrews were the ones who actually introduced into Western thought the idea of an irreversible history. History for them was a "meaning"; it is a time of fulfillment in which the present marks a progress with regard to the past, and in which the fullness of being lies in the future.

Teilhard and Mounier are once again in complete agreement. It was necessary, the latter wrote, "to awaken from their dogmatic slumber those who confused eternity with atemporality and ended up by eternalizing the present, provisional universe instead of helping to actualize the eternal in time. This error seemed to him all the more deplorable in that it made unthinkable any transformation of a social or economic system which deprived the person of his full rights.

History is one, because humanity is one. It was sin which introduced the division and led to individualism, and Christ is the one who "gathers together this dispersed humanity." Thus both sacred and secular history form but one history: that of humanity on the march, body and soul, toward the kingdom of God already present in this history. For Mounier, the idea of progressive development is the direct product of Christianity. The Eternal, according to the Christian view, transcends the world but is not separate from it; we can see, then, in this directed movement of history "a progressive liberation of man." Teilhard and Mounier keenly felt that the person can find his fulfillment only in an absolute person, that time has consistency only if it is inserted into eternity, that history has meaning only if there is something beyond history.

But at this point new questions arise. The personalist thinker, like every philosopher of history, must confront the real forces of optimism and of pessimism. Wishing to take into account the totality of that existence in which the person finds his expression, he necessarily comes up against questions arising from the tragic situations and anxieties so common in today's world.

Existentialist thought has given eloquent expression to this anguish of a world which has lost all security, this anguish of an existence devoid of all meaning and reduced to absurdity. Mounier and Teilhard set themselves the task of helping men regain their zest for life; it was to this end that they sought to revive an indispensable faith in the hearts of men. For in this hypothesis of unbelief, there remains only the "anguish

of feeling oneself enclosed in the cosmic
bubble, not so much spatially as ontologi-
cally."

The great concern therefore is to break
the circle, find an outlet, free oneself from
the net. Teilhard wanted to see and have
others see and not dream. But is not the
child terrified when he is brutally confronted with space-time, or with the world
of the machine? By an intuition independent of all "existentialist" content in the
technical sense of the term, Teilhard perceives "human anxiety as . . . bound up
with the very appearance of reflection."
Such is the condition of the person discovering his frailty. He speaks of "this fundamental anguish of the being . . . who takes
his origin in that pressure of collapse and of
uselessness, in the face of cosmic enormi-
ties." But for him, all this results from an
overly narrow view. If thought "unhesitat-
ingly follows through its intuition logically,
it perceives the evolution which animates
time and space." These latter are frighten-
ing only by their apparent immobility. But
both may become humanized, and then
only the desperate can say "nothing under
the sun has changed, nothing changes any
more."

To discover a universe in genesis, in becoming, is to transform anxiety into joy.

But "will tomorrow still move?" Teilhard's whole ambition is to show how nonsensical it would be to refuse to see the way out before us, rich as it is with the most sublime reasons for hope. In this way men will regain the desire to live and thus be able to collaborate in the work still to be done. Optimism—that is, the right to hope—is the reward of those who will give all they have. The entire history of life manifests "critical points along the way." But halt or regression seem impossible.

It is a question then of choosing. But the choice presupposes a certain faith in a "survival"—an assurance that nothing of one's personal being will ever be lost. In a word, the hypothesis of a total death must be thrust aside.

Father Teilhard de Chardin's inestimable contribution to Christian personalism has been to show that scientific reflection gives a new foundation to this philosophical or religious choice. The fact of evolution, that extraordinary success, is opposed to a philosophy of the absurd. Teilhard was certainly aware of the tragic risks involved at each stage of this totalization, this amorization. But for him love was stronger than hatred.

There is a difference of perspective, of point of view, between Mounier and Teilhard. Let us try to be more specific. The existence of the person spans, as it were, three levels of reality. First, there is the cosmological level, where man is part of the vital stream. This paleontology and biology study. It is of this temporality that Genesis speaks of when it says "God saw that it was good."

At the summit, there is the Christic level, that of temporality as preparing another, absolutely new City, the one we touched on in our discussion of the progressive building up of the Mystical Body.

Between these two, we have the historical plane in which our present existence unfolds.

Father Teilhard's thought is concerned mainly with the first two levels, both of which revealed to him the successful advance of creation toward a goal. The successful progress of life lends certitude to the scholar's research, whereas the ultimate success of Christ lends a different type of certitude to the faith of the believer. This is the basis of Teilhard's optimism. He attained, ultimately, a "perception of a closer connection between the triumph of Christ and the success of the work which human effort strives to accomplish here below." Success, therefore, and optimism, are guaranteed by the bond between christogenesis and cosmogenesis.

Teilhard dealt less systematically with the level of duration, properly so-called, which may be called "time of freedom." He certainly knew that the mystery of history is the mystery of freedom—that the latter ushers in an inescapable contingency and risk of failure. The whole process is not absolutely predestined, as we have already pointed out, and each human will can refuse to cooperate. The time of history is therefore also the time of sin. Now, this is the level with which Mounier deals most extensively, without, for all that, losing sight of Christic temporality. But given his emphasis, we can understand why he had a keener vision than Teilhard of evil and suffering, a keener sense of life's incertitudes and ambiguities. "The course of sacred history," he said, "is like the current of slow waters. We know they flow and toward what seas they flow, but we do not manage to see the exact point toward which they flow, or, therefore, in precisely which direction they flow toward that point." "Christian hope," he added, "lives from despair to despair."

And so, on the one hand, Mounier, while assigning an end to history, takes away none of the tragic grandeur of the human adventure. Teilhard, on the other hand, stresses a necessary optimism. He has told us elsewhere that he tried to bring out in bold relief the point which to him seemed more especially necessary or new, without there being any need to stress those which were all too evident. There are differences between these two thinkers. We feel that Mounier is particularly close to the social struggles without being submerged in them, whereas Teilhard is more especially bound by the austere joy of scientific research. But both lived an intense interior life, and it was this mystic depth, this community of lived faith, which gave each the wealth of insight by which he complemented the other.

The legend of the naive optimism of Father Teilhard is utterly gratuitous; he, no less than Mounier, may be said to have been characterized by what the latter called "tragic optimism." For all through the struggles and the catastrophies of history, there remains the risk of mankind's failure, refusal to embrace its destiny, and actual resignation to an unfulfilled existence. The thought of these two men is *tragic*, because they were lucidly conscious of all that this construction of the future will meet by way of obstacles to surmount, of struggles to engage in, temporary failures to undergo. Yet it is an *optimism,* because ultimate success is assured. "If the absurd cultural maelstrom in which we are caught" seems to dehumanize us more than it ultra-humanizes us, our solution lies, not in despair but rather in reexamining ourselves. It is not the inherent energy of human evolution that is at fault, but simply our manner of directing it.

If the person can only find, beyond every temptation to despair and beyond every danger that lies in the path of his progress, a solid foundation for hope, he will taste that joy, the cultivation of which "remains the most divine of duties . . . which alone lifts up and nourishes, helps us mature and sweeps us along, generates courageous optimism, and forms an integral part of human activity." To attain this joy, the person need only ascend high enough to see beyond the superficial disorder of details.

A study of the temporality of the person cannot, of course, obviate the parallel need to study the question of the person's *future.* For Mounier, as for Teilhard, this final success is positively guaranteed "by the quickening power of God incarnated in his creation." Theirs is an eschatological humanism, the flame of which is kindled by their perception, already mentioned, of the intimate bond "between the triumph of Christ, already achieved by the resurrection, and the success of the work which human effort strives to accomplish here below."

In 1933, Mounier challenged those for whom "the kingdom of God is not of this world," for whom this world is corrupt and to be avoided: "the Incarnation?" he asked them, "and the promises? and hope? The idea of a solidarity between the destiny of the universe and that of man is an idea familiar to the Fathers of the Church."

Unmitigated materialism, left to itself, ultimately destroys the person. One can and must accept many of its less extreme insights, however, and personalism shows how this can be done; the Spirit must be seen as the guiding Power, in the heart of the historical process, and history itself must be seen to be quickened by a Supreme Presence.

VII
Two Witnesses

We have attempted to give a brief outline of a few of the fundamental themes of personalist thought, specifically those which characterize the writings of Emmanuel Mounier and Father Teilhard de Chardin. The person has become visible to us: incorporated, communitarian, involved, free, of a supereminent value, centered on a supreme Person in which he finds his harmony, his energy, and his fulfillment. Without losing sight of the differences between these two scholars, to whom we are so indebted, we have seen that to a great extent they were of one mind. We have sought only to show how their thought converges in a Christian personalism—especially how Teilhard, having used his original methodology to discover the concrete preoccupations of contemporary man, harmonized them in a vision well suited to our age which is so restless and yet so promising.

It would not suffice to explain this doctrinal convergence of Mounier and Teilhard by their common religious faith, which is so rich as to be susceptible of widely varying modes of implementation. Surely the opposition of many Christians to the thought of these two men shows that their common insight cannot be identified with their faith. Yet the intensity of their adherence to Christ, bound indissolubly to an exquisite sensitivity to historical process, enabled them to explain the conditions under which this world in the making would remain under the guidance of the Spirit.

Since these reflections have been written, critics have arisen to censure Teilhard in the name of fidelity to the personalism of Mounier. This may well surprise us. It is strange, for example, that Teilhard should be blamed for having stressed both the person's immersion in nature and his uniqueness. Surely every serious effort to understand men has entailed facing up to this inadequacy of thought to cope with a reality which escapes "perfect" conceptualization. The person is "out of kilter," the only being in the world who refuses to be what he is, as Camus would say. "Cartesian" dualism (but not Descartes) is unsatisfactory. And it is characteristic of every existential attitude to set itself up as a paradox.

The permanence of the biological in man by no means deprives him of this originality of spirit. It is perhaps easier to speak of a pure spirit, but the freedom of man takes root in a "cosmic" substructure that cannot be destroyed without destroying freedom itself. And this difficulty of conceiving man is compounded when we try to conceive becoming: the history of Man, like that of every man, is that of the conquest of "matter" by spirit, undoubtedly less an obstacle than a point of departure.

It is likewise unfair to reproach Teilhard for looking at things "from above" and apparently disregarding "evil" in Simon Weil's sense. Teilhard de Chardin affirmed his optimism, his faith in the final triumph of Creation precisely in the face of his own real restlessness, and he felt keenly the price men would probably have to pay for that triumph. Is it indeed possible to give oneself over to action seeing only the evil in the world or, on the contrary, must we not discern in events, however tragic they are, the meaning which is transparently inscribed within them?

It is because he helps us to raise our eyes higher that Teilhard enables us to return and immerse ourselves in everyday life with renewed enthusiasm. He never sought to help us elude the tragic; on the contrary, the constant affirmation of "technological optimism" is matched by equally prevalent reminders of our responsibility and the need to use that responsibility wisely for our fulfillment as persons.

To take evolution in hand demands that here and now, in our daily living, we make the forces of creation prevail over those of disintegration. It is up to us to see to it that the forces of love direct those of mechanization. Not just any union is capable of furthering the process of differentiation. Without a personal effort grounded in the love of a Person greater than self, the "cosmopithecus," the "planetary man" runs the risk of being only a banal, standardized man. Convergence will stifle man if the conditions are not fulfilled which will assure his emergence into a personal authenticity.

We can see, then, the inaccuracy of such a statement as "Teilhard will never offer us the means of living our present correctly." Many people already, in fact, penetrated with his thought, are translating it into their daily actions, on the humblest level of society as well as in the midst of the most exalted responsibilities. Teilhard, like Mounier, gives no recipe for action. He offers far more: a mind capable of shedding light on every situation in which we find ourselves and of giving direction to our action. The preceding pages are not sufficient to bring this out. Only direct familiarity with his writings will throw light on this.

We are face to face with two complementary vocations inserted in the same vital current, both oriented toward a renewal of the world in the service of the human person. We have not spoken of the men that Teilhard and Mounier were. Their personalities remain implicit in the writings which have brought their message to the world. But some day the kindred inspiration of these two great minds—the kindred concerns of these two great hearts—will have to be explored. Certainly both were consumed, interiorly, by the same fire—and they were men of fire, tortured by the need to speak, in order to awaken other men to that light which cannot be extinguished for eyes which have once contemplated it. A few days before his death, Teilhard wrote: "the truth need appear but once in one mind. Nothing can then prevent it from invading everything and inflaming everything."

They were, above all else, witnesses. For Mounier, witness is an essential form of effective living. "A life that has borne a great witness is never destroyed." And witnessing is always an act of rupture with a world that stifles truth, that imprisons this truth which the witness has the mission to proclaim. The values at stake here are those of the person. And these values are fragile and constantly exposed to the forces of lethargy and egoism. One of truth's noblest functions is to bring together great minds. For truth unifies: this is what explains these encounters. We have here a beautiful illustration of the famous phrase that can well be said to summarize the entire message of Father Teilhard de Chardin: "All that ascends converges."

They were also prophets, in the sense of one who bears witness to essential values, and is thereby alone capable of building the future. The prophet, wrote Mounier, "hurls the strength of his faith before him, assured that if it does not reach some immediate goal, it will at least succeed in maintaining the vital energy of man on the only level where the vistas of history ever develop." It would be difficult to say of which one of them this statement is more true. Both were "good laborers," genuine sons of heaven, fully sons of the earth, of the earth which they so desired to perfect by transforming it. All that remains to be done is to pursue their work.